DAILEY INSPIRATION

For Women

by

AuroraDawn

Table of Contents

Chapter One	Daily Affirmations (30 Days)
Chapter Two	Inspirational Sayings
Chapter Three	Daily Motivator (20 Days)
Chapter Four	Meditations

Chapter One   Daily Affirmations

These are Daily Affirmations for 30 days. It is said it takes about 15 days to develop a habit. Change begins with our thoughts, how we think. How we see ourselves is how we will manifest ourselves. As we think so are we.

Affirmations-
They are short, powerful statements. When you say them or think them or even hear them, they become the thoughts that create your reality. Affirmations, then, are your conscious thoughts. Every thought you think every word you say is an affirmation All of our self-talk or inner dialogue is a stream of affirmations. We are continually affirming subconsciously with our words and thoughts and this flow of affirmations is creating our life experience in every moment. Our beliefs are just learned thought patterns that we have developed since childhood, many of these work well for us, but others may now be working against us, they are dysfunctional and may be sabotaging us from achieving what we believe we want. Every affirmation we think or say is a reflection of our inner truth or beliefs. It is important to realize that many of these "inner truths" may not actually be true for us now or may be based on invalid or inappropriate impressions we constructed as children, which if examined as an adult can be exposed as inappropriate.

Our subconscious uses the behaviour patterns we have learned to automatically respond and react to many everyday events in our life. This is essential to our survival, we need to be able to respond quickly to events around us which would be impossible if we had to re-examine every aspect of things every time something simple happens. Our learned responses and thought patterns enable us to automatically respond to circumstances quickly and easily. Problems arise however, if at an early stage some of the foundation beliefs on which many of the others are built were formed from a skewed perspective, maybe the strategy was appropriate for a perceived difficult circumstance, however often such beliefs are totally inappropriate for succeeding in the real world as adults.

You can use "Positive Affirmations", which are usually short positive statements targeted at a specific subconscious set of beliefs, to challenge and undermine negative beliefs and to replace them with positive self-nurturing beliefs. It is a kind of "brainwashing" only you get to choose which negative beliefs to wash away. The way these statements are constructed is extremely important. Later I will show you how to construct you own affirmations. It is important to remember of course that everything we say and think is a positive affirmation, using positive affirmation statements forces us to keep focussed on our inner goals and reminds us to think consciously about our words and thoughts and to modify them to reflect our positive affirmation.

By choosing to think and say positive affirmations as true, the subconscious is forced into one of two reactions - avoidance or reappraisal. The bigger the issue the bigger the gap between the positive affirmation and the perceived inner truth and the more likely that one is going to experience resistance. This is where the subconscious finds it easier to stay with its perceived inner truth and avoid the challenge using any means at its disposal to avoid examining the issue. You will recognise this reaction by a strong negative feeling inside as you state the positive affirmations. Equally if your experience a sense of joy and well being, your mind is instinctively responding to something it believes to be true. When you get this emotion, you know your affirmations are working!

Continually repeating affirmations with conviction and passion will chip away at even the strongest resistance. However there are a number of additional techniques you can use that will super-charge your affirmations and magnify their effectiveness many fold. I will outline these techniques for you later. Once the resistance is broken, your subconscious is able to re-examine the core belief and patterns you have been working on. The effect can be startling and things can change very quickly as the dysfunctional beliefs get identified and replaced by your own new inner truth. Depending on how deep into your consciousness these beliefs lay, every other learned pattern and belief that relied on the original belief as a premise, becomes unfounded. The subconscious has to re-examine them all, this can lead to a period of introspection. If you find yourself experiencing serious resistance or have identified an area of trauma in your life, I strongly urge you to seek professional support, the journey you are embarking on will release you from the past but having proper support around you as you go through the process will make it so much easier.

Because affirmations actually reprogram your thought patterns, they change the way you think and feel about things, and because you have replaced dysfunctional beliefs with your own new positive beliefs, positive change comes easily and naturally. This will start to reflect in your external life, you will start to experience seismic changes for the better in many aspects of your life.

Change never happens over night, but over time. Now let us begin 30 days of Affirmations

Day 1   Affirmation

I am beautiful inside, and out!

Beauty is more than skin deep. True beauty comes from within, and manifests outward. Look in a mirror at yourself, look into your own eyes and declare " I am beautiful! I am Beautiful inside and out! Choose to put all other thinking a side focus and declare I am beautiful! I am beautiful inside and out! Repeat this over and over a few times through this day. At the beginning and end of day make sure you look into your mirror so you can look into your eyes and declare_____ out loud

Day 2 Affirmation

I am sacred! I am a manifestation of the divine! I am created in the divine image.

It is written, so God created them, male and female in His own image and likeness. You have eternal value   In the beginning of this day and at the end use a mirror, and look into your eyes and declare- I am sacred! I am a manifestation of the divine! I am created in the divine image. Repeat this affirmation several times, and do so through the day out loud.

Day 3 Affirmation

I am Love. I am loved by my creator, I am full of Love, I live in Love.

Since I am in the image of my creator who is Love, and I am loved by my creator it stands to reason I am the manifestation of Love. Live in love, walk in love. Look into the mirror in the morning and end of day, and look into your eyes, declare out loud; I am Love, I am Loved, I am full of Love, I live in Love!. Declare this through the day, not based on how you feel, or on how others act.

Day 4 Affirmation

I am healthy, I live a healthy life, I am health I choose health.

Each Morning or beginning of your day, stand in front of the mirror, look into your eyes, and look at your body .Declare out loud I am Healthy, I live a healthy life, I am health. Repeat throughout the day. At end of day as you bathe look at yourself, and body and repeat again. Each time you're tempted for that food you know you do not need, repeat. When hungry for that little snack, repeat I choose health.

Day 5 Affirmation

I am Peace. I am Peace, and therefore I am at peace in all things.

Let the peace of the divine fill you. No one can take your peace. Look at yourself in the mirror eye to eye, and say I am Peace. I am Peace, and therefore am at peace in all things. No one can take my peace, for I am Peace. Repeat often out loud.

Day 6 Affirmation

I am Joy. I radiate Joy wherever I go.

Joy cometh in the morning time, unlike happiness it is not based on circumstances. It is a choice. Today choose joy. Repeat out loud several times through the day I am Joy, I am Joy filled, I radiate Joy. Practice smiling. Think on what brings you joy. Keep declaring I am Joy, I radiate Joy. I am joy filled because I am joy.

Day 7 Affirmation

I am prosperous. I am prosperous in relationships, in work, and in all I do

Prosperity is more than money, and stuff. It is being healthy so that you can do all that you desire to do. To be what you want. It is flourishing, and thriving in all you do. It is being happy with who you are, and what you have. Look at yourself in the mirror; declare out loud through your day, I am Prosperous. Prosperity follows me wherever I go. In all I do I prosper.

Day 8 Affirmation

I am a Success; Success follows me wherever I go. I am a Success in all I put my hand to.

Look in the mirror; begin the day, declaring I am a success. I am a success. I succeed in all I do. Today is a successful day because I am a success. Repeat through your day. Success is who I am; Success follows me where ever I go.

Day 9 Affirmation

I am favored I walk in divine favor; I am have favor before all.

Created in the divine image, walking in the divine likeness, you also walk in the divine favor. Begin today looking at yourself, declare I am favored, I walk in divine favor, I have favor before all. Know if you walk in the light then light will surround you.

Day 10 Affirmation

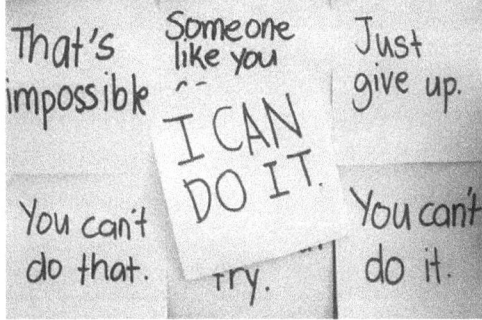

I can do all things, I can do this, I can do it,

I can do all things through Christ who strengthens me. I can do all because of the divine within me. I am made in the image of the Creator. I can do it. Make this your declaration in the beginning of your day, and throughout. Speak it out loud. You have the final say on how your day, and life will go. Declare I can do. Possess the I can attitude, and spirit, and speak it.

Day 11 Affirmation

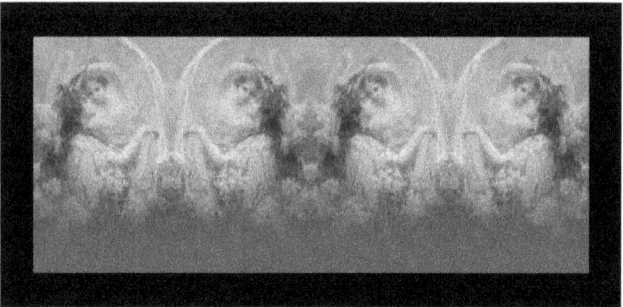

I am Blessed, I am a Blessing.

Begin the day, first count your blessings. Then declare out loud I am blessed, I am blessed, I am blessed. Today declare I am blessed, I am a blessings wherever I am. I am blessed going out and coming in. I am blessed in all I do today. I am blessed to be a blessing. Today expect opportunities to be a blessing.

Day 12 Affirmation

慷慨

Generosity

I am generous, generosity follows me, and generosity begets generosity.

Generosity begets generosity, give and it shall be given to you. Today, count your blessings, declare I am Blessed, I am generous, and generosity follows me. I am generous. My generosity begets generosity.

Day 13 Affirmation

I am excellent, I embody excellence, I live an excellent life

Look in the mirror and declare, I am excellent, I live excellence, My work is excellent. Repeat often out loud. It does not matter what others do, it is what you choose to do in private, and public which matters. Excellences follow me for I am excellent.

Day 14 Affirmation

I am Happy. I reflect Happy; I am a bowl of sunshine

Look at your face, declare out loud , I am Happy, I feel Happy, Today is a Happy day, I reflect Happy. Repeat. Emotions follow your thoughts and words. Your happiness, smile can affect those around you. Happy Happy Joy Joy!

Day 15 Affirmation

I am Smart, I am intelligent

As you think so you are. Being smart is more than just having a college diploma, or degree. Many are book smart, but do not use their life smarts day to day. Declare out loud and repeat, I am smart, I am intelligent. Never say of yourself I am stupid. Repeat out loud I am smart, I am intelligent

Day 16 Affirmation

I am rich, I am blessed, My needs are met

Rich does not mean if you affirm you become wealthy, it is a lot of work, and balancing your finances. Being responsible with what you have. If you are being responsible, working hard, then go ahead use this affirmation. I am rich, I have more than enough. My needs are met. Repeat often, speak it out loud. See yourself with more than enough.

Day 17 Affirmation

I am strong, I have strength. I am powerful

Made in the image of the Creator, you are powerful; you are stronger than what you think. Today is a day of power, of strength. Declare out loud and repeat often, I am strong, I am powerful, I have strength. Remember the Divine spirit, essence, image in you. I am the image of my creator, I am strong, I am powerful.
(Note No you're not all powerful)

Day 18 Affirmation

I am Humble, and therefore not easily offended

Blessed are the Meek for they will inherit the earth, Pride comes before a fall. Our Creator resists the proud, but gives grace, favor to the humble. Declare this day I am humble. I am humble and do not walk in offence I am humble, and therefore not easily offended.

Personal Growth Affirmations

Day 19 Affirmation

Self esteem

I love and accept myself. I understand and accept that my imperfection makes me perfect. Therefore, I am perfect exactly as I am and will remain perfect as I learn and grow.

Hug embraces you in front of a mirror. Look at yourself and say out loud I love and accept myself. I understand and accept that my imperfection makes me perfect. Therefore, I am perfect exactly as I am and will remain perfect as I learn and grow.

Repeat and do this several times today

Day 20 Affirmation

Releasing the past affirmation

All things happen for a purpose. My past experiences also had purpose. ¬? I have learned from my past and am now free from it. I choose to release the past and live in the now. I completely release the past and live in the now.

Know this there is no accidents, and your life has a purpose. Today declare- Today is a new beginning. All things happen for a purpose. My past experiences also had purpose. ¬? I have learned from my past and am now free from it. I choose to release the past and live in the now. I completely release the past and live in the now.

Day 21 Affirmation

Forgiveness

I have been forgiven, therefore I forgive others.

Work or School Affirmations

Day 22 Affirmation

I am the image of the creator, therefore I am creative, and creative energies flow through me.

In the Mirror, as you dress speak out loud I am not tired. I am the image of the creator, therefore I am creative, and creative energies flow through me. I am full of life, and energy. Repeat often.

Day 23 Affirmation

I am the best me, I give 100 percent in all I do.

Declare this often today.

Day 24 Affirmation

I am orderly, organized

Declare today you are orderly, organized. You complete assignments on time Begin your day, and repeat this through your day.

Affirmations for the Spirit

Day 25 Affirmation

I am the gardener who has nurtured my body and soul with essential nutrients and a healthy lifestyle. Much like the saying "April Showers Bring May Flowers" I am enjoying the fruits of my own care taking. Everything in my life is coming up daisies!

Day 26 Affirmation

I am the spirit, soul, and body. I am balanced within, and without. I am whole within, and without. I am healthy within, and without.

Day 27 Affirmation

I am a person of faith. I walk by faith, I live by faith. No one, no circumstance can take my faith away.

Day 28 Affirmation

I am a radiant being of Light and Love.

I am Divinity in the flesh.

Day 29 Affirmation

I am free of the past and the future.

The moment I live in is now, with no history affecting my choices in the present.

Day 30 Affirmation

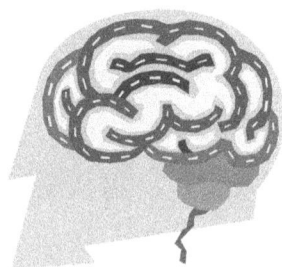

*I remember myself as the master that I am,
the master I have always been.*

*I have mastery over my life by
how still I can keep my mind and how
alert I am in the now.*

Chapter 2 Inspirational Sayings

1. Leadership quotes-

Courage is courageous. When a brave man takes a stand, the spines of others are stiffened.
- Reverend Billy Graham, author and evangelist

Leaders become great, not because of their power, but because of their ability to empower others.
- Author John C. Maxwell

Look at adversity as an opportunity to discover your strengths because there are opportunities galore out there. Thomas Edison said it well, 'If you did all the things in life you were truly capable of, you would astound yourself.'
- Nadja Piatka, Founder of Nadja Foods

My purpose is to serve, and not be served
  - Jesus Christ

Where there is no vision, the people perish. —Proverbs 29:18

Never doubt that a small group of thoughtful, concerned citizens can change world. Indeed it is the only thing that ever has. —Margaret Mead

A leader takes people where they want to go. A great leader takes people where they don't necessarily want to go, but ought to be. —Rosalynn Carter

Do what you feel in your heart to be right–for you'll be criticized anyway. —Eleanor Roosevelt

It is better to lead from behind and to put others in front, especially when you celebrate victory when nice things occur. You take the front line when there is danger. Then people will appreciate your leadership. —Nelson Mandela

Lead and inspire people. Don't try to manage and manipulate people. Inventories can be managed but people must be lead. —Ross Perot

Leaders aren't born, they are made. And they are made just like anything else, through hard work. And that's the price we'll have to pay to achieve that goal, or any goal. —Vince Lombardi

2. Inspiring Quotes from Great Women in History

"We never know how high we are
Till we are called to rise;
And then, if we are true to plan,
Our statures touch the skies."
— Emily Dickinson, American poet

"Aging is not 'lost youth' but a new stage of opportunity and strength."
— Betty Friedan, author of "The Feminine Mystique"

"I have learned over the years that when one's mind is made up, this diminishes fear; knowing what must be done does away with fear."
— Rosa Parks, African-American civil rights activist

Leadership is a series of behaviors rather than a role for heroes.
Margaret Wheatley (1941-), American social scientist, systems manager, educator, author. From "The Unplanned" (pp. 17-23), Noetic Sciences Review, Spring 1996

Leave the fishing-rod, Great General, to us sovereigns of Pharos and Canopus. Your game is cities and kings and continents.
Cleopatra VII (69 B.C.E.-30 C.E.), Egyptian queen. From Cleopatra of Egypt by Philip W. Sergeant; Remark to Marc Antony, Quoted in Ch. 9

"What the world needs," he said, "is not a Joan of Arc, the kind of woman who allows herself to be burned on the cross. That's just a bourgeois invention meant to frighten little girls into staying home. What we require is a real female military social leader."
"But that" -- I smiled at him -- "is just impossible. Women are tied to husband and children. Women are constructed to be penetrated; a sword or a gun in their hands is a joke or a mistake. They are open holes in which things are poured. Occasionally, it's true, a woman can become a volcano, but that's about it."
Anne Roiphe (1935-), American novelist. From "Out of Week Two," Up the Sandbox!, 1970

Professional intellectuals are the voice of a culture and are, therefore, its leaders, its integrators and its bodyguards.
Ayn Rand (1905-1982), Russian-American novelist, philosopher, screenwriter; devised philosophy of "objectivism". From For the New Intellectual, 1961

The more princes abstain from touching the wealth of their people, the greater will be their resources in the wants of the state.
Aelia Pulcheria (399-454), Byzantine scholar, empress saint; canonized by the Greek Orthodox Church. Quoted in Biography of Distinguished Women by Sarah Josepha Hale, 1876

Being consistent meant not departing from convictions already formulated; being a leader meant making other persons accept these convictions. It was a narrow track, and a one-way, but a person might travel a considerable distance on it. A number of dictators have.
Jessamyn West (1902-1984) American novelist. From To See the Dream, Ch. 7, 1956

And the propensity of weak and empty people to follow a leader into the darkness from which there is no return is still flourishing, as ever.
Mary McGrory (1918-2004) American Pulitzer Prize-winning columnist. From "Holocaust Museum holds appalling relevance today," Seattle Post-Intelligencer, Op-Ed, 27 April 1993

...the discontent of the people is more dangerous to a monarch than all the might of his enemies on the battlefield.

Isabella d' Este (1474-1530), Italian noble, art patron. From letter to her husband (Milan, February 1495), Quoted in Beatrice d'Este by Julia Cartwright, 1899

Perhaps the seeds of false-refinement, immorality, and vanity, have ever been shed by the great. Weak, artificial beings, raised above the common wants and defections of their race, in a premature and unnatural manner, undermine the very foundation of virtue, and spread corruption through the whole mass of society!
Mary Wollstonecraft (1759-1797), English feminist, author. From Introduction to A Vindication of the Rights of Women, 1792

He is a leader of darkness and death... You can see his cowardice. Moi* is playing a game alone. He is player and referee.
Charity Kaluki Ngilu (1952-), Kenyan politician; MP. Quoted in "Kenya's First Woman President?" by Andrea Useem, Ms. (New York), November/December 1997. * Ref. Daniel arap Moi, president of Kenya (1978-2002).

[Margaret] Thatcher had just become prime minister; there was talk about whether it was an advance to have a woman prime minister if it was someone with policies like hers: She may be a woman but she isn't a sister, she may be a sister but she isn't a comrade.
Caryl Churchill (1938-), English playwright; winner of three Obies and the Society of West End Theatre Award, 1988. From "Caryl Churchill," Interviews with Contemporary Women by Kathleen Betsko and Rachel Koenig, 1987

I might not be someone's first choice, but I am a great choice.
I may not be rich but I am valuable.
I don't pretend to be someone I'm not, because I'm good at being me.
I might not be proud of some of the things I've done in the past, but I am proud of who I am today.
I may not be perfect but I don't need to be. Take me as I am, or watch me as I walk away.

Chapter 3 Daily Motivator

Day 1- It is ok to Cry

We are human. I am and so are you. We all have emotions. Sometimes healing comes quicker when we allow ourselves a good cry. We as women are naturally more emotional. Yet as many are professionals "We just don't cry, at least not in public" Ok understandable. But when is last time you went to a dear friend honestly, and just said I need a good cry. Tears do not make you weak. Tears sometimes are the best stress release. Many times we do not cry because of ego. It is the weak who allow their ego to rule them.

Day 2- The way up is down
Promotions in life often are hard to come by. Sometimes to us it is not fair.
There is a wise saying; The person who wishes to be great must first be the servant, the one who wishes to be first must be willing to be last" The path to promotion is the path of humility. For pride comes before a fall. Seek ways to humble yourself, and watch in time see if promotion does not come your way.

Day 3 – I cannot afford I can't
You and I cannot afford to waste energy on I can't. Truth is I will not. If you believe you cannot then you will not. Be careful with whom you hang around. We want honest but positive people in our lives. What we feed in our lives will grow. Think I can, speak I can I will I am.

Day 4 – The Law of Attraction
We attract whatever we think about, good or bad. Oprah is a fan of the law and devoted an episode of her show to how it could change lives. Whether or not you believe in the power of the universe, there is scientific research that proves the effects of positive thinking.

Day 5- The Four Agreements
The Four Agreements are:
Author- Miguel Ruiz

1. Be Impeccable with your Word: Speak with integrity. Say only what you mean. Avoid using the Word to speak against yourself or to gossip about others. Use the power of your Word in the direction of truth and love.

2. Don't Take Anything Personally
Nothing others do is because of you. What others say and do is a projection of their own reality, their own dream. When you are immune to the opinions and actions of others, you won't be the victim of needless suffering.

3. Don't Make Assumptions
Find the courage to ask questions and to express what you really want. Communicate with others as clearly as you can to avoid misunderstandings, sadness and drama. With just this one agreement, you can completely transform your life.

4. Always Do Your Best
Your best is going to change from moment to moment; it will be different when you are healthy as opposed to sick. Under any circumstance, simply do your best, and you will avoid self-judgment, self-abuse, and regret.

Day 6 – Forgiveness

It is funny how we want forgiveness for ourselves, but when it is time for us to forgive we have issues. If we do not forgive we are forever bonded to the person we refuse to forgive. Forgiveness opens the door for bitterness. Bitterness is poison, and will poison all your relationships as well. If you want forgiveness, then you must yourself be willing to forgive.

Day 7- Happiness is every person's choice, but few make an effort for it.

Choose today to smile, think happy thoughts. Feelings follow our thoughts. Positive thinking will bring positive emotions. Think happy thoughts today. Think, and count your blessings. We all have things, and people we can be grateful for. Remember the movie, or story of Peter Pan, happy thoughts made him fly.

Day 8- The Slip of the Tongue

How often we are too quick to speak, and slow to really listen. Result is we fall for foot in mouth syndrome or we allow words to slip otherwise we would never speak. We have two ears, one mouth my mom has many times reminded me as I grew up. There is a difference in hearing, and listening. We can hear words but never listen.

Day 9 – Making things Matter

When everything is free and instantly available, nothing matters. It is only when you must work for something that it becomes important. It seems nice to imagine a life completely free of challenges. Yet such a life would be utterly and painfully meaningless.It is what you put into life that makes life good for you. It is what you give of yourself that gives real meaning to whatever you experience. Keep in mind that you must venture in order to experience adventure. You must give in order to know how truly great it is to live. Don't waste your time wishing in vain for a life free of effort. Instead, invest your precious time in loving, meaningful, value-creating, life-enhancing activities.

Make the commitment, invest the time, and do the work to make things matter. Your life has magnificent potential, so with your efforts give it the substance and meaning it deserves.

— Ralph Marston

Day 10- Excuses

Leadership - leadership is about taking responsibility, not making excuses.
Mitt Romney
Not managing your time and making excuses are two bad habits. Don't put them both together by claiming you 'don't have the time'. When you hear the word "responsibility," what do you think of first? Many people think of the word BLAME, as in, "Whose responsibility is this?" I'd like to instead suggest that you think of responsibility as seizing what's in front of you, exerting choice, and taking control. The real meaning of responsibility is the ability to respond. It's going out and creating what you want through personal choices.

Day 11 – Temptation

Definition : a strong urge or desire to have or do something

: something that causes a strong urge or desire to have or do something and especially something that is bad, wrong, or unwise
The truth about temptation is, most of us have not even made an honest attempt at resisting temptation. We cave in immediately without much of a fight. "Well, I'll quit doing that next week." "Why struggle now when I know I am going to do it again anyway?" "It is just a matter of time, and now is as good a time as any." But temptation feeds on weakness and bent desires. We need to start struggling to see what holiness is all about, to see if we will like it in eternity with God. We will also see just how strong we are and what we are made of.

*I Fall, I Rise,
I make mistakes,
I Live,
I learn, I've been hurt,
but I'm Alive.
I'm Human and
I'm not perfect but
I'm Thankful...*

www.wisdomquotesandstories.com

Day 12- Enjoy the Real you

Enjoy being the real you

Fear is the enemy of creativity. If you are anxious and worried about what you are creating, then what you are creating will not be worth very much.
Let go of your attachment to getting it right. Allow yourself to enjoy the experience of simply letting it flow. When you are truly having fun you can create magnificent things. When you stop worrying about whether people will like it, people will love it.The way to be great is to be authentic. The way to be authentic is to enjoy who you truly are and what you truly love. Don't waste a lot of time trying to guess what might matter to someone else. Put your love and effort and energy into what matters to you, and many others will benefit.

In order to give of yourself you must fully be yourself. Enjoy being the real you, and bring great value to life.

— Ralph Marston

Day 13 – Gratitude

Today be thankful. Focus on what you do have, not on what you do not. Gratitude is a matter of attitude, and a choice. Your attitude determines your altitude in life. Choose to be thankful. Express your gratitude to others. What we take for granted we often loose. It is written some place, In everything give thanks, for this is the will of God. Gratitude will keep you from the drippy attitude of complaining too.

Day 14 – Drip Drip

It is said that constant complaining is like a continually dripping of water. Constant complaining feeds negative energy, and it is what repels people away. It is irritating, and contagious. So is gratitude. Contagious. Choose with your thoughts and words to not go complaining. Do not be a drip.

Day 15 – I dare you

Do something Different than you have ever done before. It has been said it is the fool who does things the same old way yet expects different results. Time to try something new, or old, but different. I dare you.

Day 16- Courage

fearlessness, dauntlessness, intrepidity, pluck, spirit. Courage, bravery, valor, bravado refer to qualities of spirit and conduct. Courage permits one to face extreme dangers and difficulties without fear: to take (or lose) courage. Bravery implies true courage with daring and an intrepid boldness: bravery in a battle. Valor implies heroic courage: valor in fighting for the right. Bravado is now usually a boastful and ostentatious pretense of courage or bravery: empty bravado. If you will to soar in life, you must have courage.
Courage is
Feeling Fear Yet Choosing to Act
Following Your Heart
Standing Up For What Is Right

Day 17 – A Freudian slip

A Freudian slip is a verbal or memory mistake that is believed to be linked to the unconscious mind . Words reveal what is in our hearts. It is said out of the abundance of the heart the mouth speaks or out of the sub consciousness of the heart words come. Believe it or not we mean more than what we think we do. Our words even a slip reveal what is going on inside. I think we would shock ourselves if our words were recorded for 24 hour period.

Day 18 – Authentic living

Authentic living Do you wish to be truly rich? Then be truly you.

Your greatest asset is the unique person you are. Make full and positive use of it to make life truly rich and fulfilling.Anything you gain through deception is not really a gain at all. It adds nothing to the richness that you seek.Instead of striving to acquire unfair advantage, make use of the immense, authentic advantage you already have. Make use of your valuable perspective as the unique, authentic person you are.You have great value, so live it. You have the potential for immense richness, so allow it to come through authentic living.Give the best of who you are, of what you have, in the service of what you love. That will make your life rich beyond all measure.

— Ralph Marston

Day 19 – What is your plan?

"If you don't design your own life plan,
chances are you'll fall into someone else's plan.
And guess what they have planned for you?
Not much."

~ Jim Rohn

Day 20 - Treat yourself

Today treat yourself to something good Pamper you. Often we are consumed by taking care of everyone else and feel guilty if we want a break .It is time for you treat yourself kindly. If you do not take time for you, what good will you be when you burn out. Refresh, and refill yourself. You will be glad you did. Maybe it is time to go to the Spa, or go get your hair, nails done. Find something you really enjoy and do it. Get away from the daily today.

Chapter 4 Meditations

1. Christian Mediation

Christian Meditation: Is it Christian to Meditate?
Christian meditation is rooted in the Bible. In fact, the Bible commands us to meditate. In Joshua 1:8, God says to meditate on His word day and night so we will obey it. The psalmist says "his delight is in the law of the Lord, and in His law he meditates day and night" (Psalm 1:2). Actually, the Bible mentions meditate or meditation 20 times.

In the Old Testament there are two primary Hebrew words for meditation: Haga, which means to utter, groan, meditate, or ponder; and Sihach, which means to muse, rehearse in one's mind, or contemplate. These words can also be translated as dwell, diligently consider, and heed.
Meditation for Christians

© 2012 Phil Fox Rose — Rock and Water, Onteora Lake, Kingston, NY
With most spiritual matters I say different things might work best for different people, but I have no reservations saying everyone should meditate. Regular meditation is invaluable in aligning with God's Will, with the way things are — however you want to say it — and by so doing, in reducing anxiety and self-driven suffering. It changes you.
The promise of a devoted spiritual life, of which meditation is an invaluable part, is serenity — not that nothing bad will ever happen but that you will be able to walk through setbacks, disappointments and even outright tragedies carried by a trust that things will be OK; that in everyday life you will not be anxious, restless or irritable; and that in good times you will be fully alive to enjoy them.
There are many forms of meditation. I believe Centering Prayer is particularly good for cultivating radical acceptance, but if a different practice speaks to you, consider that. I discourage you, though, from any practice that's goal-oriented, complicated or overly attached to form, or which has an underlying philosophy that repeatedly contradicts your beliefs. As Thomas Merton said,
"Contemplative prayer has to be always very simple, confined to the simplest of acts." If you don't know where to start, I offer this simple framework from my centering prayer tradition.

Centering prayer really has just one action: When you realize you're engaged with a thought, you let it go. That's it. No special postures, breathing patterns or mantras.

Most people find it helpful to use a word of one or two syllables — when they realize they've gotten caught up in a thought, they say the word to themselves silently as they let go of the thought and return to God's presence. Some examples of words are: Amen, Abba, Grace, Love, Oneness, Peace, Let Go, Silence, Stillness, Jesus. Pick one thoughtfully, but don't get hung up on it. This is not a sacred mantra that is supposed to have meaning in itself. At first you may want to try different words. That's fine. Just don't change it within a session. Some prefer to use a simple inward glance toward the Divine Presence, or noticing one's breath.

Resist no thought; retain no thought; react to no thought. When you realize you are engaged with a thought, return gently to the stillness. Centering prayer is not about pushing thoughts away, or trying diligently to have no thoughts. Our minds were designed to have thoughts. As Rev. Cynthia Bourgeault says, "striving for emptiness is a surefire way to guarantee that your meditation will be a constant stream of thoughts." In centering prayer, we let thoughts happen, but we don't engage them. We let them float by without giving them attention, and, before you know it, they're gone.

You may drift into not needing the word, just "resting in God." This is wonderful when it happens, but it's not the goal and it won't last. With practice, the clutter in your head will reduce, but you may stay in the attachment-surrender loop for an entire session. That's OK too. As Fr. Thomas Keating says, ten thousand thoughts are "ten thousand opportunities to return to God."

Sit comfortably, feet planted on the ground and back supported — so there is no need to adjust while sitting, and to encourage alertness. Sit for 20 minutes or more if at all possible. Something often happens to the stillness around 10 to 15 minutes in. If you stop too soon you will miss it.

Set a timer. You set it and then can turn to sitting until it goes off. Having to check a clock or watch is distracting. After maybe an opening tone or reading, settle briefly, and silently introduce the sacred word to start the sitting period; repeat it for a few minutes, or a few times, then let go of it and rest in the silence. If you realize you've been focused on a thought, let it go, say the word to yourself or notice your breath, and return to the silence. When the ending bell sounds, take a minute or two to gradually return to ordinary awareness. Don't hop right up. Many practitioners say a closing prayer

2. The Chakras

The word chakra is derived from the Sanskrit word meaning wheel. If we were able to see the chakras (as many psychics, in fact, do) we would observe a wheel of energy continuously revolving or rotating. Clairvoyants perceive chakras as colorful wheels or flowers with a hub in the center. The chakras begin at the base of the spine and finish at the top of the head. Though fixed in the central spinal column they are located on both the front and back of the body, and work through it.

Each chakra vibrates or rotates at a different speed. The root or first chakra rotates at the slowest speed, the crown or seventh chakra at the highest speed. Each chakra is stimulated by its own and complimentary color, and a range of gemstones for specific uses. The chakra colors are of the rainbow; red, orange, yellow, green, blue, indigo, and violet. The size and brightness of the wheels vary with individual development, physical condition, energy levels, disease, or stress.

If the chakras are not balanced, or if the energies are blocked, the basic life force will be slowed down. The individual may feel listless, tired, out of sorts, or depressed. Not only will physical bodily functions be affected so diseases may manifest, but the thought processes and the mind may also be affected. A negative attitude, fear, doubt, etc. may preoccupy the individual.

A constant balance between the chakras promotes health and a sense of well being. If the chakras are opened to much, a person could literally short circuit themselves with too much universal energy going through the body. If the chakras are closed, this does not allow for the universal energy to flow through them properly which may also lead to dis-ease.

Most of us react to unpleasant experiences by blocking our feeling and stopping a great deal of our natural energy flow. This affects the maturation and development of the chakras. Whenever a person blocks whatever experience he is having, he in turn blocks his chakras, which eventually become disfigured. When the chakras are functioning normally, each will be open, spinning clockwise to metabolize the particular energies needed from the universal energy field.

THE SEVEN MAJOR CHAKRAS

First Chakra - Root

Studying the individual chakras begins with the root chakra, called Muladhara in Sanskrit. The root chakra is located at the base of the spine at the tailbone in back, and the pubic bone in front. This center holds the basic needs for survival, security and safety. The root chakra is powerfully related to our contact with the Earth Mother, providing us with the ability to be grounded into the earth plane. This is also the center of manifestation. When you are trying to make things happen in the material world, business or material possessions, the energy to succeed will come from the first chakra. If this chakra is blocked an individual may feel fearful, anxious, insecure and frustrated. Problems like obesity, anorexia nervosa, and knee troubles can occur. Root body parts include the hips, legs, lower back and sexual organs. The colors used for this chakra are red, brown and black. The gemstones are Garnet, Smoky Quartz, Obsidian, and Black Tourmaline. NOTE: A man's sexual organs are located primarily in his first chakra, so male sexual energy is usually experienced primarily as physical. A women's sexual organs are located primarily in her second chakra, so female sexual energy is usually experienced primarily as emotional. Both chakras are associated with sexual energy

Second Chakra - Belly (Sacral)

The second chakra is often referred to as the belly or sacral chakra. It is located two inches below the navel and is rooted into the spine. This center holds the basic needs for sexuality, creativity, intuition, and self-worth. This chakra is also about friendliness, creativity, and emotions. It governs peoples sense of self-worth, their confidence in their own creativity, and their ability to relate to others in an open and friendly way. It's influenced by how emotions were expressed or repressed in the family during childhood. Proper balance in this chakra means the ability to flow with emotions freely and to feel and reach out to others sexually or not. If this chakra is blocked a person may feel emotionally explosive, manipulative, obsessed with thoughts of sex or may lack energy. Physical problems may include, kidney weakness, stiff lower back, constipation, and muscle spasms. Belly body parts include sexual organs (women), kidneys, bladder, and large intestine. The main color used with this chakra is orange. The gemstones are Carnelian Agate, Orange Calcite and Tigers Eye.

Third Chakra - Solar Plexus

The third chakra is referred to as the solar plexus chakra. It is located two inches below the breastbone in the center behind the stomach. The third chakra is the center of personal power, the place of ego , of passions, impulses, anger and strength. It is also the center for astral travel and astral influences, receptivity of spirit guides and for psychic development. When the Third Chakra is out of balance you may lack confidence, be confused, worry about what others think, feel that others are controlling your life, and may be depressed. Physical problems may include digestive difficulties, liver problems, diabetes, nervous exhaustion, and food allergies. When balanced you may feel cheerful, outgoing, have self-respect, expressive, enjoy taking on new challenges, and have a strong sense of personal power. The body parts for this chakra include the stomach, liver, gall bladder, pancreas, and small intestine. The main color for this chakra is yellow. The gemstones are Citrine, Topaz, and Yellow Calcite.

Fourth Chakra - Heart

The fourth chakra is referred to as the heart chakra. It is located behind the breast bone in front and on the spine between the shoulder blades in back. This is the center for love, compassion and spirituality. This center directs one's ability to love themselves and others, to give and to receive love. This is also the chakra connecting body and mind with spirit. Almost everyone today has a hard, hurt, or broken heart, and it is no accident that heart disease is the number one killer in America today. Deep heart hurts can result in aura obstructions called heart scars. When these scars are released, they raise a lot of old pain, but free the heart for healing and new growth. When this chakra is out of balance you may feel sorry for yourself, paranoid, indecisive, afraid of letting go, afraid of getting hurt, or unworthy of love. Physical illnesses include heart attack, high blood pressure, insomnia, and difficult in breathing. When this chakra is balanced you may feel compassionate, friendly, empathetic, desire to nurture others and see the good in everyone. Body parts for the fourth chakra include heart, lungs, circulatory system, shoulders, and upper back. The main colors used are pink and green. The gemstones are Rose Quartz, Kunzite, and Watermelon tourmaline.

Fifth Chakra - Throat

The fifth chakra is referred to as the throat chakra. It is located in the V of the collarbone at the lower neck and is the center of communication, sound, and expression of creativity via thought , speech, and writing. The possibility for change, transformation and healing are located here. The throat is where anger is stored and finally let go of. When this chakra is out of balance you may want to hold back, feel timid, be quiet, feel weak, or can't express your thoughts. Physical illnesses or ailments include, hyperthyroid, skin irritations, ear infections, sore throat, inflammations, and back pain. When this chakra is balanced you may feel balanced, centered, musically or artistically inspired, and may be a good speaker. Body parts for the fifth chakra are throat, neck, teeth, ears, and thyroid gland. The main color used is light blue. The gemstones are Aquamarine and Azurite.

Sixth Chakra - Third Eye

The sixth chakra is referred to as the third eye or brow chakra. It is located above the physical eyes on the center of the forehead. This is the center for psychic ability, higher intuition, the energies of spirit and light. It also assists in the purification of negative tendencies and in the elimination of selfish attitudes. Through the power of the sixth chakra, you can receive guidance, channel, and tune into your Higher Self. When this chakra is not balanced you may feel non-assertive, afraid of success, or go the opposite way and be egotistical. Physical symptoms may include headaches, blurred vision, blindness, and eyestrain. When this chakra is balanced and open you are your own master with no fear of death, are not attached to material things, may experience telepathy, astral travel, and past lives. Sixth chakra body parts include the eyes, face, brain, lymphatic and endocrine system. The main colors are purple and dark blue. The gemstones are Amethyst, Sodalite, and Lapis Lazuli.

Seventh Chakra - Crown

The seventh chakra is referred to as the crown chakra. It is located just behind the top of the skull. It is the center of spirituality, enlightenment, dynamic thought and energy. It allows for the inward flow of wisdom, and brings the gift of cosmic consciousness. This is also the center of connectedness with the Goddess (God), the place where life animates the physical body. The silver cord that connects the aura bodies extends from the crown. The soul comes into the body through the crown at birth and leaves from the crown at death. When this chakra is unbalanced there may be a constant sense of frustration, no spark of joy, and destructive feelings. Illnesses may include migraine headaches and depression. Balanced energy in this chakra may include the ability to open up to the Divine and total access to the unconscious and subconscious. The main colors for the crown are white and purple. The gemstones are Clear Quartz Crystal, Oregon Opal, and Amethyst.

Source for the Chakras-
The Seven Major Chakras
Study of the Chakras

By Kellie Jo Conn, GG Holelistic Healing

3. Buddhist Meditation
Lamrim: The Stages of the Buddhist Path

In general, any virtuous object can be used as an object of meditation. If we discover that by acquainting our mind with a particular object our mind becomes more peaceful and virtuous, this indicates that for us that object is virtuous. If the opposite happens, for us it is a non-virtuous object. Many objects are neutral and have no particular positive or negative effect on our mind.

If we appreciate the great potential of this life we shall not waste it
There are many different virtuous objects of meditation. By relying upon a qualified Spiritual Guide we open the door to practising Dharma. Through the blessings of our Spiritual Guide we generate faith and confidence in our practice, and easily attain all the realizations of the stages of the path. For these reasons we need to meditate on relying upon a Spiritual Guide. We need to meditate on our precious human life to realize that we now have a special opportunity to practise Dharma. If we appreciate the great potential of this life we shall not waste it by engaging in meaningless activities.

We need to meditate on love, compassion....
and develop and maintain a good heart towards all living beings.

We need to meditate on death and impermanence to overcome procrastination, and to ensure that our Dharma practice is pure by overcoming our preoccupation with worldly concerns. If we practise Dharma purely it is not very difficult to attain realizations. By meditating on the danger of lower rebirth, taking refuge sincerely, and avoiding non-virtue and practising virtue, we protect ourself from taking lower rebirth and ensure that life after life we shall obtain a precious human rebirth endowed with all the conditions conducive to the practice of Dharma.
We need to meditate on the sufferings of humans and gods so that we develop a spontaneous wish to attain permanent liberation, or nirvana. This wish, known as 'renunciation', strongly encourages us to complete the practice of the spiritual paths, which are the actual methods for attaining full liberation.

We need to meditate on love, compassion, and bodhichitta so that we can overcome our self-cherishing and develop and maintain a good heart towards all living beings. With this good heart we need to meditate on tranquil abiding and superior seeing so that we can eradicate our ignorance and finally become a Buddha by abandoning the two types of obstruction.

What is the goal of meditation?

Through analytical meditation we shall perceive our object clearly, then through placement meditation we shall gain deeper levels of experience or realization. The main purpose of all Lamrim meditations is to transform our mind into the path to enlightenment by bringing about the deepest levels of realization. The sign that we have gained perfect realization of any object is that none of our subsequent actions are incompatible with it and that all of them become more meaningful. For example, when we have gained a perfect realization of compassion we are never again capable of willingly inflicting harm upon any other living being and all our subsequent actions are influenced by compassion.

Simple Breathing Meditation

The first stage of meditation is to stop distractions and make our mind clearer and more lucid. This can be accomplished by practising a simple breathing meditation. We choose a quiet place to meditate and sit in a comfortable position. We can sit in the traditional cross-legged posture or in any other position that is comfortable. If we wish, we can sit in a chair. The most important thing is to keep our back straight to prevent our mind from becoming sluggish or sleepy.

The first stage of meditation is to stop distractions and make our mind clearer and more lucid.
We sit with our eyes partially closed and turn our attention to our breathing. We breathe naturally, preferably through the nostrils, without attempting to control our breath, and we try to become aware of the sensation of the breath as it enters and leaves the nostrils. This sensation is our object of meditation. We should try to concentrate on it to the exclusion of everything else.

At first, our mind will be very busy, and we might even feel that the meditation is making our mind busier; but in reality we are just becoming more aware of how busy our mind actually is. There will be a great temptation to follow the different thoughts as they arise, but we should resist this and remain focused single-pointedly on the sensation of the breath. If we discover that our mind has wandered and is following our thoughts, we should immediately return it to the breath. We should repeat this as many times as necessary until the mind settles on the breath.

Benefits of Meditation

If we practise patiently in this way, gradually our distracting thoughts will subside and we will experience a sense of inner peace and relaxation. Our mind will feel lucid and spacious and we will feel refreshed. When the sea is rough, sediment is churned up and the water becomes murky, but when the wind dies down the mud gradually settles and the water becomes clear. In a similar way, when the otherwise incessant flow of our distracting thoughts is calmed through concentrating on the breath, our mind becomes unusually lucid and clear. We should stay with this state of mental calm for a while.
Even though breathing meditation is only a preliminary stage of meditation, it can be quite powerful. We can see from this practice that it is possible to experience inner peace and contentment just by controlling the mind, without having to depend at all upon external conditions.

So much of the stress and tension we normally experience comes from our mind When the turbulence of distracting thoughts subsides and our mind becomes still, a deep happiness and contentment naturally arises from within. This feeling of contentment and well-being helps us to cope with the busyness and difficulties of daily life. So much of the stress and tension we normally experience comes from our mind, and many of the problems we experience, including ill health, are caused or aggravated by this stress. Just by doing breathing meditation for ten or fifteen minutes each day, we will be able to reduce this stress. We will experience a calm, spacious feeling in the mind, and many of our usual problems will fall away. Difficult situations will become easier to deal with, we will naturally feel warm and well disposed towards other people, and our relationships with others will gradually improve.

Source - © 2012 How to Meditate.
The New Kadampa Tradition – International Buddhist Union ~ Kadampa.org
Kadampa Buddhism is an international Buddhist tradition, presenting pure and authentic teachings in a manner suitable for the modern world.

Tharpa Publications International ~ Tharpa.com

Books and audiobooks on Buddhism and meditation which offer something for everyone.
Tharpa books are written by Geshe Kelsang Gyatso, the fully accomplished meditation master and internationally renowned teacher of Buddhism.
Tharpa also publishes Buddhist Art and Buddhist Prayers.
All Tharpa profits are donated to the NKT-International Temples Project, a Nonprofit Buddhist Organization Building for World Peace.

Kadampa Festivals ~ kadampafestivals.org

More Buddhist Websites

Living Meditation – simple meditations for everyday life ~ daily-meditations.com
About Buddhism ~ aboutbuddhism.org
About Buddha ~ aboutbuddha.org
About Dharma ~ aboutdharma.org
About Meditation ~ aboutmeditation.org
About Tantra ~ about-tantra.org
About Reincarnation ~ aboutreincarnation.org
Anger Management Techniques ~ anger-management-techniques.org
Find Happiness ~ findhappiness.org
How to Meditate ~ how-to-meditate.org
Death and Dying ~ death-and-dying.org
Dealing with Fear ~ dealingwithfear.org
Find Peace of Mind ~ findpeaceofmind.org
Learn Meditation Techniques ~ learn-meditation-techniques.org

www.ingramcontent.com/pod-product-compliance
Lightning Source LLC
Chambersburg PA
CBHW032012080426
42735CB00007B/585